EXTREME WORLD

THE WORLD'S WILDEST WEATHER

by Laura K. Murray

raintree
Capstone company — publishers for children

Raintree is an imprint of Capstone Global Library Limited, a company incorporated in England and Wales having its registered office at 264 Banbury Road, Oxford, OX2 7DY – Registered company number: 6695582

www.raintree.co.uk
myorders@raintree.co.uk

ISBN 978 1 3982 4763 5 (hardback)
ISBN 978 1 3982 4764 2 (paperback)

Editorial Credits
Editor: Christopher Harbo; Designer: Kay Fraser; Media Researcher: Svetlana Zhurkin; Production Specialist: Katy LaVigne

Image Credits
Getty Images: Cultura RM Exclusive/Jason Persoff Stormdoctor, cover, 1, EasyBuy4u, 5, Roberto Machado Noa, 12, Warren Faidley, 13; NOAA Weather in Focus Photo Contest 2015: Ken Engquist, 8; Shutterstock: Da-ga, 20 (bottom right), Kichigin, 14, Milju Varghese, 11, Minerva Studio, 7, Rainer Lesniewski, 9, Realstock, 19, RicardoJara, 18, Rininii, 15, Rob Byron, 21, RTimages, 20 (top), Szasz-Fabian Ilka Erika, 20 (bottom left), Vadym Gryga, 16, valdezrl, 6, Vitaliy Kaplin, 17

All internet sites appearing in back matter were available and accurate when this book was sent to press.

British Library Cataloguing in Publication Data
A full catalogue record for this book is available from the British Library.

Printed and bound in India.

CONTENTS

Words in **bold** are in the glossary.

WILD WEATHER

Lightning flashes in the sky. Snow falls fast and hard. **Tornadoes** twist along the ground. The world's weather can be wild! Sometimes it is dangerous too. From **hurricanes** to **blizzards**, Earth has so much weather to explore.

THUNDERSTORMS

Right now, about 2,000 thunderstorms are happening around the world. They create bright lightning, loud thunder and strong winds. They can also drop heavy rain.

Supercell

The strongest thunderstorms are called supercells. Their clouds tower high in the air. They can drop **hail** the size of tennis balls!

TORNADOES

Some thunderstorms make tornadoes. A tornado is a spinning tube of air. It forms between a cloud and the ground. Its winds can lift buildings, cars and trees!

Each year, the United States has about 1,200 tornadoes. Many form in an area called Tornado Alley. It stretches from Texas to Minnesota.

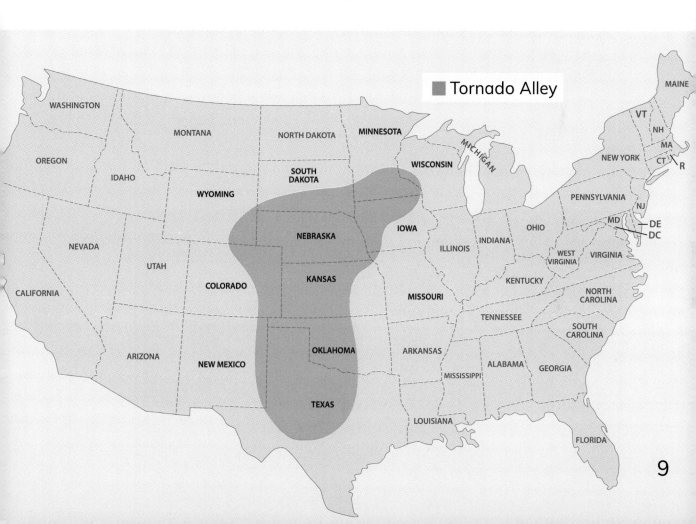

MONSOONS

Wind can create a lot of wild weather. Parts of Asia and Africa have **monsoon** seasons. Monsoons happen when strong winds change direction.

Monsoons bring very wet or very dry weather. In the wet season, monsoons bring heavy rain and flooding. Some areas get most of their rain in just a few months.

11

HURRICANES

Hurricanes are huge spinning storms. They form over warm ocean waters. The middle of a hurricane is called the eye. Rainbands spin around the eye.

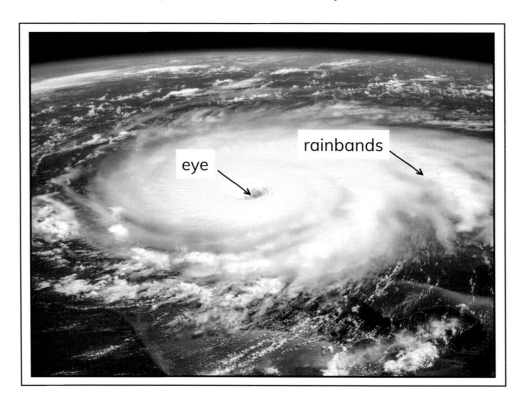

eye

rainbands

Hurricanes bring high winds and heavy rain. Their strong winds can push big waves ashore. These **storm surges** can flood whole cities.

SNOW

Wild weather often includes snow. Snow forms when water freezes in the clouds. The water turns into ice **crystals** that stick together. No two snowflakes are the same.

The Japanese Alps get the most snow. Up to 38 metres (125 feet) of snow falls each year. That is enough snow to bury an eight-storey building!

BLIZZARDS

Blizzards are very dangerous winter storms. Their high winds whip falling snow all around. Temperatures often drop far below freezing.

Blizzards also create huge snowdrifts and blinding **whiteouts**. Snowdrifts can bury roads and cars. Whiteouts make it hard to see anything around you.

DROUGHTS

Sometimes wild weather means no water at all. Droughts are dry spells that last months or years. The ground dries up. Plants and animals die without water.

From thunderstorms to droughts, the world has a lot of amazing weather. It changes every day. Just look out the window to see it in action!

TORNADO IN A JAR

Tornadoes form a funnel shape between clouds and the ground. Dust and other materials get caught up in the spinning air. Make your own tornado in a jar to see how it spins!

WHAT YOU NEED
- plastic or glass jar with a lid
- water
- measuring spoons
- liquid soap
- vinegar
- food colouring
- glitter (optional)

WHAT YOU DO

1. Fill the jar with cold water. Leave about 2.5 centimetres (1 inch) of space at the top.

2. Add 1 teaspoon of liquid soap to the jar.

3. Add 1 teaspoon of vinegar to the jar.

4. Add a few drops of food colouring. If you like, also add a pinch of glitter to represent dust.

5. Put the lid on the jar. Make sure it's sealed tight.

6. Hold the jar by the lid. Swirl the jar in a small circle so everything mixes together. Watch your tornado funnel form!

GLOSSARY

blizzard a heavy snowstorm with strong wind; a blizzard can last several days

crystal when a substance changes from liquid to solid, crystals can form. Their shapes have patterns.

hail balls of ice that can fall during thunderstorms

hurricane a very large storm with high winds and rain; hurricanes form over warm ocean water

monsoon a very strong seasonal wind that brings heavy rains or hot, dry weather

storm surge a sudden, strong rush of water that happens as a hurricane moves onto land

tornado a violent spinning column of air that makes contact with the ground

whiteout blowing snow that makes it difficult or impossible to see objects in the distance

READ MORE

BOOKS

The Brainiacs Book of the Climate and Weather, Rosie Cooper (Thames and Hudson, 2022)

What Are Hurricanes? (Wicked Weather), Mari Schuh (Raintree, 2020)

What Are Tornadoes? (Wicked Weather), Mari Schuh (Raintree, 2020)

WEBSITES

NASA's Climate Kids
climatekids.nasa.gov/menu/weather-and-climate

National Geographic Kids: Hurricane
kids.nationalgeographic.com/science/article/hurricane

ABOUT THE AUTHOR

Laura K. Murray is a USA-based author of more than 90 published or forthcoming books for young readers. She loves learning from fellow readers and helping others find their reading superpowers! Visit her at LauraKMurray.com.

INDEX